RAND

Data Cleaning Procedures for the 1993 Robert Wood Johnson Foundation Employer Health Insurance Survey

Roald Euller, Stephen H. Long,
M. Susan Marquis

Supported by
The Robert Wood Johnson Foundation

PREFACE

This report documents the procedures for data cleaning and imputation for the 1993 Robert Wood Johnson Foundation Employer Health Insurance Survey. The survey was conducted in 10 states to provide state-level data on the employment-based health insurance market. RAND designed the survey under a grant from The Robert Wood Johnson Foundation's State Initiatives in Health Care Reform program.

The authors are very grateful to Linda Andrews, who carried out much of the cleaning and imputing for the surveys from the public employers. We thank David Adamson who reviewed an earlier draft of this report and made many helpful organizational and structural suggestions. We also thank state policy analysts in the states in which surveys were conducted, whose use of early versions of the data files helped us identify problems with the files and design procedures to fix them. Finally, we thank Joan Keesey for her technical review of a draft of this manuscript.

CONTENTS

FIGURE

TABLES

1. INTRODUCTION

PURPOSE OF THIS REPORT

The 1993 Robert Wood Johnson Foundation (RWJF) Employer Health Insurance Survey was a part of the Foundation's State Initiatives in Health Care Reform program, which provides funding and technical assistance to states developing and undertaking reforms to expand health insurance coverage. The survey, conducted in ten states, was designed to assist states in defining problems with their employment-based health insurance markets and in analyzing the impacts of policy options.

The RWJF survey was designed by RAND. Westat, in Rockville, MD, conducted the interviews. Details about the survey methods are reported elsewhere.[1] The purpose of this report is to describe the methods RAND used to clean the data prior to distributing analysis files to the participating states and releasing public-use files to the research community. The goal of the data cleaning was to remove some response error and to reduce bias from item nonresponse. We detail our methods here to provide a record of the adjustments that we have made for other users of these data.

The rest of this section briefly describes the survey. The next section provides an overview of our objectives in editing the data and imputing for missing or edited values. The remainder of the report describes the specific procedures that were used to clean the data.

BACKGROUND ON THE SURVEY

The purpose of the RWJF survey was to provide the ten states with information to:
- Describe the existing employment-based insurance system and its problems
- Conduct prospective policy analysis of alternative proposals to expand access to employment-based insurance
- Provide a baseline against which to measure the effects of new policies and programs after they are implemented.

In addition, the Foundation viewed this as an opportunity to develop a standard set of instruments and procedures for employer health insurance surveys that might be adopted by other states or researchers.

---

[1]Westat, Inc., "Robert Wood Johnson Foundation Employer Survey: Data Collection Methodology Report," report submitted to the Robert Wood Johnson Foundation, April 1995.

The survey was conducted in the latter half of 1993 and early 1994 in Colorado, Florida, Minnesota, New Mexico, New York, North Dakota, Oklahoma, Oregon, Vermont, and Washington. Separate frames, or sampling lists, were used to select private and public employers.

Approximately 2,000 thirty-minute telephone interviews were conducted with private employment establishments in each state. An establishment—a physical location of business—was the sample unit. Because our objective was to make state estimates, we sampled a unit that was contained within state borders. In eight of ten states, the sample was selected from Dun & Bradstreet's Market Identifiers (DMI) file, a national census of employment establishments. In the remaining two states,[2] the sample was selected from the state unemployment insurance files. Because many of the reforms that states were considering focused on small employers, the private establishment sample in each state was allocated equally to four strata defined by the number of employees at the establishment (1–4, 5–9, 10–24, and 25 or more).[3]

Public employers were also interviewed. The objective was to survey health insurance purchasing units for public employers, which may represent many government agencies or departments, rather than to select individual government agencies or subunits. Therefore, Westat constructed a sample frame for each state in consultation with representatives from the state and other governmental units. Large purchasing units, such as all state employees and the largest counties and municipalities, were selected with certainty. The number of public-sector purchasing units selected varied among the states from 46 to 255. Public-sector purchasing units were mailed a self-administered questionnaire; nonresponding units were contacted by phone, and interviewers attempted to complete the questionnaires by telephone.

---

[2]Minnesota and Oregon.

[3]The probability of selection for establishments of 25 or more employees was proportionate to the number of employees in the establishment.

2. PURPOSES OF EDITING AND IMPUTING

Editing refers to the process of screening responses for implausible values. Imputing refers to the process of replacing missing or implausible values for an observation with plausible values; these are typically estimated from other observations in the sample. Both of these processes are intended to reduce bias in population estimates. Editing and imputing are closely related. If a record fails an edit, we replace it with an imputed value. In addition, imputed values must be examined to ensure that they pass the edit screens.

Editing is an effort to identify and remove some of the response error in surveys. Response error can arise for a number of reasons, including data entry error, respondent misunderstanding, and intentional misreporting. Response error is an important potential source of bias in estimates made from surveys. Our editing procedures are not intended to eliminate all response error from the data, but rather intended to eliminate extreme or outlier values that may have an unduly large effect on estimates of mean values or relationships among variables.

Imputing is done to correct for bias that may arise from item nonresponse in surveys.[4] Biased estimates of population parameters will result if sample units report a value different from those that fail to report a value. For example, an estimate of the average annual deductible in employer health insurance policies based only on observed values will be an underestimate of the population value if those with high deductibles fail to report the amount. Imputing can correct for this type of bias if we are able to identify correlates of nonresponse that are also associated with the value of the missing item. For example, if the size of the deductible differs among industries and if nonresponse about the amount of the deductible varies among industries, we might be able to reduce bias due to item nonresponse by using this information. Notice that doing nothing about missing data items and simply discarding these cases in analysis adopts the implicit assumption that there are no differences between responders and nonresponders.[5]

As an alternative to imputing, analysts can correct for item-nonresponse bias in analysis by using existing data and positing an appropriate model for the nonresponse. The imputation process is in fact a process of adopting a model of nonresponse. The advantage of imputing for the

---

[4]Survey nonresponse, which occurs when the sample observation does not complete an interview, may also produce bias. We correct for this type of nonresponse by weighting. Weighting is discussed in detail in the Westat field methodology report (op. cit.).

[5]Even if this assumption is true, failure to impute for missing data will produce biased estimates of aggregates because the sum of the weights applied to the cases with data present will not equal the sum of the weights applied to all cases, which is the measure of the total population size.

missing data is that it produces a complete data set from which different analysts can easily produce population estimates with consistent nonresponse assumptions.

In choosing imputation techniques, we want procedures that will preserve the underlying distribution of the data and preserve relationships among variables. Different techniques vary in how well they do this. For example, the technique of replacing all missing values for a variable with the mean value for responding cases might distort the distribution of values and the estimate of the relationship between the variables and other measures unless only a very small amount of data is imputed. On the other hand, taking account of a large number of related variables in imputing for a missing item usually involves strong model assumptions. We adopt several different techniques in our imputation. These are described in the following sections. The choice of technique for any particular variable depends on how much information is missing (and so how influential the imputed values may be in estimating population parameters), on the number of related variables for which we have measures, and on our confidence in adopting particular models describing a characteristic.

3. METHODS

In this section, we describe the generic techniques that we adopted for editing and imputing data. In the following two sections, we discuss the imputation and editing techniques for specific variables.

EDITING

We edited the data to identify "outlier" values and to identify responses to a question that were inconsistent with responses to other questions. Outlier values and inconsistent responses were then adjusted or imputed as described later in this section.

Outlier Values

An outlier is a response on a single variable that falls outside of the established range of legitimate values for that variable. We established ranges to identify outliers that would preserve as much of the reported data as possible while eliminating extremes on the observed distribution of responses. Table 1 shows the outlier cutoff points. These outlier checks were applied prior to imputation and again after new values were imputed to ensure that the new values did not violate our criteria.

Table 1

Values Established as Out-of-Range or Outliers

Variable (Question #)[a]	Outlier Value
Payroll hours (D34)	Average hours per week <10 or > 70 hours
Single premium	Monthly premium <$40 or >$1,000
Family premium	Monthly premium <$60 or >$1,500
Employer share of premium	Share > 100 percent
Employee share of premium[b]	Share > 100 percent
Deductible (C20)	Deductible <$50 or >$5,000
Copayment (C23)	Copayment >$50 per visit
Stop-loss (C25)	Stop-loss <$100 (for HMOs) Stop-loss <$100 or >$25,000 (non-HMOs)

[a] Refers to numbering in the questionnaire, where applicable.
[b] Used only to determine employer share when missing. Does not appear on analysis file.

Inconsistent Responses

We edited the data for two types of inconsistent responses. The first type occurs when components do not add to totals. An example of this is when the reported numbers of workers in different age and sex groups do not sum to the total number of workers reported in another question. Another example is when the sum of the reported number of current employees enrolled in each different health insurance plan offered differs from the numbers of current employees reported to be enrolled in all of the employer's plans. Typically, such inconsistencies were corrected by "rescaling" the component parts to the total. For example, we would accept the reported total number of workers and adjust the reported number of workers in each age and sex subgroup by multiplying the reported responses by a constant factor so that the adjusted sum corresponds to the total number of workers.

The second type of inconsistent response occurs when the value of a variable falls outside of a specified relationship with other variables. An example occurs when the reported total payroll is large relative to the number of workers, implying an excessively large payroll per worker. Edits of this type are analogous to screening for outlier values, except that responses to more than one question are taken into account in comparing the value to an established upper or lower bound. Table 2 gives the out-of-range values that we established as evidence of inconsistent responses.

Table 2

Values Established for Inconsistent Responses

Variable (Question #)	Inconsistent Response Value
Payroll (D33)	Average annual salary (D33/number of workers) <$1,000 or >$300,000
	Average hourly wage (D33/payroll hours) <$2 or >$150
Family premium-to-single premium ratio	Ratio < 1.0 or > 10.0
Annual premiums-to-payroll ratio	Ratio > 0.5
Out-of-plan deductible and copayment	Could not be less than in-plan deductible or copayment
Maximum out-of-pocket	Could not be less than deductible
Employees joining (D8)	Ratio D8 to total employees > 99th percentile
Employees leaving (D10)	Ratio D10 to total employees > 99th percentile

IMPUTING

Imputing is the process of estimating values for observations that have missing or edited responses on particular items. We imputed values for sample cases that did not provide responses to particular items and for cases that failed our single or multiple variable outlier and consistency screens discussed above.

We used four methods for imputing: (1) table lookup, (2) hot deck using previously processed records, (3) hot deck using the full donor pool, and (4) regression methods. All of these methods involve grouping observations into relatively homogeneous subgroups or strata, which are then processed or treated separately. The assumption is that, within these homogeneous groups, the item to be imputed is missing at random. That is, the characteristics used to group the observations are assumed to explain the pattern of missing data. Each of the methods is discussed below.

A key objective of the imputation process was to preserve relationships between and among groups of related variables. Therefore, each of the imputation methods takes into account the values of several important characteristics related to the measure to be imputed. One implication of this is that the imputation process imposed a definite order in which certain variables were imputed. For example, we used establishment age as a stratifying or grouping variable in imputing the number of former employees currently covered by the employer's insurance plan. However, for some observations, establishment age itself required imputation. Therefore, the imputation of establishment age necessarily preceded the imputation of the number of former employees enrolled in the employer's plan. The detailed discussion in the next section attempts to preserve the actual order in which variables were imputed, because this was a central aspect of the entire process.

Each state was processed separately in imputing variables. This was done because we wanted the imputations to reflect the distribution of values within a state. However, for some variables, as indicated in the detailed discussion of the next section, the distribution of values in the ten states combined was used for imputing.

Table Lookup

This technique was used to impute categorical variables whose values vary with relatively few independent characteristics. Imputed values are assigned by comparing a random number against a table or matrix of probabilities. The matrix was stratified by characteristics—such as state, establishment size, Standard Industrial Classification (SIC) code, and establishment age—that are related to variation in the variable to be imputed. The matrix entries were the probabilities of the occurrence of the categories measured from the values of all observed, legitimate responses. Given an observation to be imputed, we first determined into which cell the observation falls, then drew a random number and compared it with the cell probability to determine the value to be assigned.

For example, we used this technique to impute answers to the question "Is this plan self-insured or fully insured?" (C14).[6] First, we constructed a matrix of the probability of being fully insured for each of six establishment size groups. For each observation to be imputed, a random number was generated. If the random number was less than or equal to the cell probability for the observation's size class, the observation was coded as fully insured. Otherwise, it was coded as being self-insured.

Hot Deck Using Previously Processed Records

"Hot deck" procedures for imputing values involve replacing a missing item using values from another record in the file. The hot deck method using previously processed records allowed us to impute variables during a single pass through the data set. Characteristics related to the variable to be imputed define a finite number of strata. As we passed through the data, the hot deck routine updated the value on the variable to be imputed for each stratum when a "clean" (i.e., nonmissing, nonoutlier) value was encountered. When a record to be imputed was encountered, it was assigned the current value for its stratum—that is, the value for the immediately preceding record belonging to the stratum.

A primary advantage of this hot deck procedure is that it is relatively undemanding in its use of resources. It requires a single pass through the data. It does not require constructing additional files or donor pools, fitting models, or generating random numbers. However, because states were imputed one at a time, this procedure limited donor records to just that one state, thus making state an implicit stratifying criterion.

Hot Deck Using Full Donor Pool

This method also imputes a value for one sample observation by replacing the missing item with the value from another sample observation in the same stratum. It differs from the preceding method in that, for each observation that is to be imputed, we randomly selected a record from among all records with "clean" data in the strata, rather than selecting the immediately preceding observation in the file.

This approach, rather than the hot deck using previously processed records, was typically used to impute variables in which state was not used as one of the stratification dimensions. When imputing variables where state was not a criterion, drawing on the entire 10-state survey made a

---

[6]Here and throughout, parenthetical letter and number combinations refer to the questionnaire number (Westat, Inc., April 1995).

much larger universe of donor records available. With a larger supply of donor records, the stratifying criteria could be more restrictive without the donor pools becoming too small, a danger if drawing from a single state only.

Regression Model

The fourth imputation strategy used a multivariate regression model. The data set was divided into two groups: the cases that have clean data on the variable to be imputed and the cases to be imputed. A regression model was fit on the first subset, where the dependent variable was the variable to be imputed. Using the fitted model, the residual distribution was generated from observations in the clean data. We used the fitted regression to predict an expected value for each observation with a missing value. A residual value was randomly drawn from the pool of residuals and added to the predicted value so that our imputed values would preserve variation around the mean value of the characteristic among similar cases. In some instances, we found that the residual distribution varied with characteristics of the establishment. In such cases, the residual values were grouped into strata, and we drew a residual from the appropriate subset of all residuals when imputing values.

An advantage of the regression model approach to imputation relative to the hot deck approach is that we can take into account a large number of important predictor variables. This is not practical or possible with hot deck techniques, because strata cell sizes would be too small or empty. However, a disadvantage of the regression model approach is that it rests on model assumptions. In contrast, the hot deck procedure does not rely on strong model assumptions and has been referred to by some as a type of "nonparametric regression."[7]

The regression imputations typically occurred at the end of the imputation process because all of the independent variables used in the regressions had to be imputed before regressions could be estimated and used to predict for the missing cases.

PRIVATE VERSUS PUBLIC ESTABLISHMENTS

The RWJ Employer survey sampled two categories of establishments: private and public. There were 22,347 private establishments and 543 public establishments surveyed. We imputed separately for these two groups. The distribution of characteristics of public and private workers differs and so it was appropriate to construct different donor pools for the groups. The discussion of imputation techniques that follows describes the imputation of variables to private establishments only. Data for public establishments were imputed using similar methods, but

---

[7]Innis G. Sande, "Hot Deck Imputation Procedures," in *Symposium on Incomplete Data*, Panel on Incomplete Data of the Committee on National Statistics, December 1979.

because of the much smaller sample size, some of the characteristics used to form the homogeneous groups were simplified. Also, public establishments tended to be atypical—for example, a state government agency with many thousands of employees—which made it difficult to create donor pools or to hot deck missing values, since there were few, if any, similar establishments to draw upon. Therefore, some characteristics that we imputed for private establishments were not imputed for public employers. A description of the imputation techniques for public establishments is located in Appendix A.

4. IMPUTATION OF ESTABLISHMENT-LEVEL VARIABLES TO PRIVATE EMPLOYERS

The specific imputation and editing of variables in the public-use data files are described in two parts. This section discusses the variables that describe the establishments that were the sample units. Each establishment that responded to the survey reported on the characteristics of each different insurance plan that was offered to employees. The next section describes the imputation methods for the insurance plan variables.

Table 3 summarizes the establishment variables for which we imputed when we encountered missing information and the specific technique we used for each. The first column of each table reports the percentage of observations providing nonmissing and nonoutlier data for the respective item. Throughout the remainder of this report, the term "clean" will refer to the subset of data with nonmissing, nonoutlier responses. More detail is provided in the discussion below.

TOTAL EMPLOYEES

National firm size (A6)—the number of employees in all establishments that are part of the parent company—was imputed using a hot deck with a donor pool stratified by establishment size and whether or not health insurance was offered (see Table 3). Less than 2 percent of the observations required imputation for this variable.

In addition to cases that failed to report the number of employees nationally, some respondents provided information about the range in which the total number of employees fell, but not the exact number. Respondents who could not report the exact number were permitted to answer the question with a bracketed response (e.g., 25–99, 100–999). For these cases, a discreet value was drawn from the observed values for establishments with a national firm size in the same range that reported the actual (unbracketed) total number of employees.[8]

EMPLOYEE CHARACTERISTICS

We imputed for the following variables describing employee characteristics when there were missing values: percent permanent/temporary workers (A11, A12); the number of workers who joined/left the establishment in the previous year (D8, D10); the number of current/former/retired workers covered by health insurance (A44, A45, A46, A48, A49); and the hours, age and sex, and wage distributions of workers (D25, D26, D27, D29/31).

---

[8]The public-use files contain indicator variables that identify, or "flag," imputed values. However, cases that assigned discreet values to bracketed responses were not flagged as imputations in the public-use file.

Table 3. Imputation Method for Establishment Variables

Imputed Variable	Percent Clean[a]	Variables Used in Imputation							Imputation Type
		State	Establishment Size[b] (A1)	SIC Code (D2)[c]	Establishment Age (D1)	Offers Health Insurance (A19)	Union (A18)	Mix of Plan Type[d] (C3)	
National firm size (A6)	98.7		x			x			HD-DP
Percent permanent employees (A11)	97.9	x	x	x					HD-PPR
Percent temporary employees (A12)	97.9	x	x	x					HD-PPR
Number employees joined in past year (D8)	94.8		x						HD-DP
Number employees left in past year (D10)	94.8		x						HD-DP
Number covered employees (A44)	97.9	x	x						HD-PPR
Number former employees covered (A45)	91.3	x			x			x	HD-PPR
Retirees eligible for coverage (A46)	95.4	x			x				TL
Number retirees over 65+ covered (A48)	95.9	x			x				HD-PPR
Number retirees under 65 covered (A49)	95.5	x			x				HD-PPR
Hours distribution permanent employees (D25)	93.3		x	x		x			HD-DP
Hours distribution temporary employees (D26)	92.4		x	x					HD-DP
Age and sex distribution of employees (D27)	86.2		x	x		x	x		HD-DP
Wage distribution of employees (D29/D31)	74.2		x	x		x	x		HD-DP
Establishment age (D1)	95.8	x	x	x					HD-PPR
Incorporated/for profit (D3/D4)	95.6		x	x					HD-DP
Payroll period (D32)	92.7		x						HD-DP

[a]Computed responses that passed our edit checks for within-range values.

[b]Size categories varied depending on the number of additional classification criteria and the resulting size of the donor pools or hot deck cells.

[c]SIC = Standard Industrial Classification code. Six industry groupings were used: manufacturing, wholesale, retail, financial, professional, and other.

[d]Establishments were characterized by the mix or combination of plan types offered. There were three plan types—HMO, PPO, and conventional plan—yielding seven possible categories.

TL = Table Lookup.

HD-PPR = Hot Deck with Previously Processed Records.

HD-DP = Hot Deck with Donor Pool.

"Clean" item response rates ranged from 74.2 to 97.9 percent.[9] Most clean response rates were over 90 percent, but there was considerable nonresponse to some of the questions concerning the distribution of workers by age and sex,s and wage.

Questions about the percentage of workers who are permanent and temporary (A11, A12) had high response rates. The cases with missing data were imputed by a hot deck with previously processed records stratified by state, establishment size, and industry (SIC) class (see Table 3).

Imputing responses to questions about the number of current, former, and retired workers covered by health insurance (A44, A45, A46, A48, A49) was more complicated because parallel versions of each question were asked at the plan level as well (C6, C7, C8, C9). This meant that the establishment-level variable and the plan-level variable had to be consistent. For example, the sum of plan enrollments (C6) across all plans for the establishment had to equal enrollment for the entire establishment (A44). Before imputing the establishment variables, we examined the parallel plan variables to determine if the equivalent but missing establishment variable could be answered directly from the plan level. If plan-level information was not complete for all plans, the establishment variable was imputed by random draw from donor pools.

The donor pools used to impute the numbers of current workers covered (A44) were stratified by establishment size and the mix of plans offered (such as HMO only or HMO and PPO).[10] Plan mix was included because it seemed likely that establishments offering similar combinations of plans would be more likely to exhibit similar distributions of enrollment across plan types. For example, an establishment offering an HMO and a PPO would be a more accurate predictor of plan enrollments in an establishment offering the same plan types but with missing enrollments than would an establishment offering PPO and conventional plans. State was an additional stratification variable.

Measures of the number of former and retired workers covered by health insurance (A46–A49) were imputed using a hot deck with previously processed records (see Table 3), stratified by state and by nine categories of establishment age (D1). Establishment age was included because older establishments are more likely to have larger numbers of covered former workers than are newer establishments. (These imputations were only done for establishments reporting that former

---

[9]That is, responses that passed our edit checks.

[10]Donor pools for A44 were stratified into two size categories (less than 10 employees, 10-plus employees), and six plan-mix categories (representing all possible combinations of the three plan types—HMO, PPO, and conventional plan). No attempt was made to distinguish between establishments offering more than one of a specific plan type: An establishment offering a PPO and an HMO was classified the same as an establishment with a PPO and three HMOs. Thus the imputation in effect drew *shares* of enrollments in each of the three plan types. Establishments with multiple plans of the same type drew an enrollment share for that plan type and then had that share apportioned randomly across the plans with missing enrollments.

workers were eligible for insurance.) The value drawn from the hot deck was the *ratio* of covered workers to establishment size: This ratio was then applied to the establishment size of the recipient record.

The clean response rate for questions about the numbers of workers joining or leaving an establishment during the preceding year (D8, D10) was 94.8 percent. Imputations were done by a random draw from the combined 10-state donor pools divided into seven categories of establishment size. Prior to imputing these variables, we flagged cases with values beyond the 99th percentile of the distribution as outliers. These outlier values were also replaced with imputed values.

Clean response rates ranged from 74.2 to 93.3 percent for the questions about the distribution of workers by age and sex, hours worked, and earnings (D25–D31). The distribution by earnings had the lowest response rate. Imputations were done by random draws from donor pools. For the hours distribution, the pool was stratified by three criteria: establishment size, industry, and whether or not health insurance was offered. To impute the age and sex distribution and wage distribution, we added union status to the list of stratification measures. We imputed percentage distributions rather than the actual numbers for all of these variables and multiplied the imputed percentage by the establishment size.

EMPLOYER CHARACTERISTICS

Imputed employer characteristics included establishment age (D1) and incorporated/for profit status (D3, D4). Clean response rates for these variables were over 95 percent. Establishment age was imputed using a hot deck with previously processed records. The hot deck was subdivided by state, size, and industry. Incorporated/for profit status is a combination of two variables from the original instrument. It was imputed using donor pools stratified into six industry groups.[11]

PAYROLL

Questions related to payroll had the lowest item response rates in the survey. Over 37 percent of respondents refused or did not know the amount of payroll (D33). Among reported values, 8 percent were flagged as outliers either in terms of average annual salary per worker or average hourly wage per worker (see Table 2). As a result, we imputed values for 45 percent of respondents. Similar nonresponse rates were observed for question D34 (total number of payroll hours), where 40 percent refused or did not know the value.

---

[11]The categories were manufacturing, wholesale, retail, financial, professional, and other.

Although the questions on the instrument asked about total payroll and total payroll hours (both for the most recent payroll), we imputed average annual pay per worker and average number of hours worked per week and multiplied the imputed values by establishment size. We did this because we have prior work to guide us in formulating models for pay per worker and average weekly hours. First, a regression model was estimated to explain pay per worker and average weekly hours. The explanatory, or independent, variables are listed in Table 4. A mean value for each charactcristic was then imputed for an establishment with a given set of independent characteristics using the estimated model. Next, residuals were drawn to reproduce variation around the mean. The residual pools were subdivided into four establishment-size categories.[12]

After imputing payroll and hours, we checked the imputed values to confirm that the imputation had not generated outliers. In some cases, it was necessary to redraw residuals to ensure this. At the completion of the entire imputation process for all variables, including premiums, a final edit check was administered: This prevented the ratio of total premiums to total payroll from exceeding 50 percent. Slightly less than 1 percent of establishments violated this last condition after premium imputation. For these cases, we redrew the payroll residual until total premiums no longer exceeded 50 percent of payroll.

Table 4

Establishment Variables Imputed Using a Regression Model

Dependent variables	annual payroll (D33)
	annual number of hours in payroll (D34)
Independent variables	state
	establishment size (A1)
	establishment age (D1)
	SIC code (D2)
	for profit (D3)
	incorporated (D4)
	other branches in U.S. (A5)
	union status (A18)
	offers health insurance (A19)
	hours distribution of permanent employees (D25)
	presence of temporary workers (D26)
	age and sex distribution of employees (D27)
	wage distribution of employees (D29/D31)
	payroll period (D32)

---

[12]The establishment size categories were 1–4, 5–9, 10–24, and 25-plus employees.

5. IMPUTATION OF HEALTH INSURANCE PLAN-LEVEL VARIABLES FOR PRIVATE EMPLOYERS

This section describes techniques for editing and imputing the variables describing each health insurance plan. Table 5 summarizes the methods, which are detailed below.

PLAN TYPE

Type of health insurance plan (C3—a categorical variable indicating whether the plan is an HMO, PPO, or a conventional plan) was imputed for 4 percent of cases. The missing values were imputed using a lookup table subdivided by state and six establishment-size categories (see Table 5). A random draw determined plan type. For a subset of the cases missing type of plan, we knew whether the plan was self-insured. Self-insured plans were not permitted to be imputed as HMOs; instead, they were only allowed to be imputed as PPOs or conventional plans. In effect, this meant that self-insured versus fully insured status was another imputation stratum.

ENROLLMENT

Plan enrollment (variable C6) was imputed for 10.4 percent of cases. Imputing plan enrollment was one of the most complex tasks of the entire imputation process, for several reasons. First, about 10 percent of the sample needed to be imputed—roughly 2,000 cases. Second, a given establishment could have several plans. For these multiplan sites, the entire set of plans was imputed simultaneously to control for total enrollment and for the distribution of enrollment across plans. This would not be possible if plan enrollments were imputed one plan at a time, because nothing would be known about the number of workers already enrolled in other plans in that establishment. Related to this was the common situation in which establishments offering multiple plans reported enrollment for some but not all of the plans offered.

The following sequence of steps was taken to impute enrollment:

1. Input total enrollment at the establishment level (see above). This provided a base or control total for the subsequent plan-level enrollment imputations.
2. For establishments with only one plan, assign plan enrollment from total enrollment.
3. For cases with enrollment missing for only one plan, assign enrollment to the missing plan subtracting the sum of known enrollments from total enrollment.
4. If all plan enrollments are known, but the sum is greater or less than the size of the establishment or total enrollment, scale or prorate plan enrollments so that their sum matches to the known (or previously imputed) total establishment enrollment figure.

Table 5. Imputation Method for Plan Variables

Imputed Variable	Percent Clean[a]	State	Establishment Size (A1)[b]	SIC Code (D2)[c]	Mix of Plan Type (C3)[d]	Union Membership (A18)	Self-Insured Status (C14)	Employer Share of Single Premium	Employer Share of Family Premium	Imputation Type
Plan type (C3)	96.0	x	x							TL
Plan enrollment (C6)	89.6	x	x							HD-DP
Number former employees enrolled (C7)	91.7	x			x					HD-PPR
Number retirees over 65 enrolled (C8)	98.5	x			x					HD-PPR
Number retirees under 65 enrolled (C9)	98.7	x			x					HD-PPR
Self-insured status (C14)	97.6	x	x							TL
Benefits: plan offers										
Prenatal care (C57a)	94.0	x	x							TL
Maternity care (C57b)	95.1	x	x							TL
Outpatient drug (C57c)	96.0	x	x							TL
Mental health (C57d)	89.9	x	x							TL
Alcohol/drugs (C57e)	87.5	x	x							TL
Dental care (C57f)	97.0	x	x							TL
Employer share of single premium	70.8	x	x	x	x	x	x		x	HD-DP
Employer share of family premium	70.	x	x	x	x	x	x	x		HD-DP
Family enrollees (C11)	83.8	x	x						x	HD-DP

[a]Computed responses that passed our edit checks for within-range values.

[b]Size categories varied depending on the number of additional classification criteria and the resulting size of the donor pools or hot deck cells.

[c]SIC = Standard Industrial Classification code. Six industry groupings were used: manufacturing, wholesale, retail, financial, professional, and other.

[d]Establishments were characterized by the mix or combination of plan types offered. There were three plan types—HMO, PPO, and conventional plan—yielding seven possible categories.

TL = Table Lookup.

HD-PPR = Hot Deck with Previously Processed Records.

HD-DP = Hot Deck with Donor Pool.

5. If all plan enrollments are missing, impute using a random draw from donor pools stratified by establishment size and seven mix-of-plan types (see Table 5). Mix-of-plan type offered—HMO, PPO, conventional plan—was an important criterion, since it permitted us to distribute the "pool" of enrollees in a manner similar to other establishments offering the same mix of plans. A simple random apportionment would not have captured this. As for the establishment variable, A44, we drew enrollment shares and multiplied them by A44 to impute the actual enrollments.

6. If some but not all plan enrollments are known, impute by drawing from donor pools stratified by size and mix of plan types, but only impute the missing plan enrollments, which get a prorated share of the remaining pool of enrollees. (The remaining pool of enrollees is total enrollment minus the sum of known plan-specific enrollments.)

COST SHARING

These variables included the deductible amount, copayment amount, coinsurance rate, and stop-loss (maximum out-of-pocket expense). For HMOs and PPOs, there were also questions about the deductible, copayment, and coinsurance rate for out-of-plan or nonpreferred provider services. Imputation rates ranged from 5.1 for nonpreferred deductible to 22.8 for stop-loss.

The guiding principle for the cost-sharing imputations was that there was a strong correlation between these variables within a given plan. Thus we imputed the cost-sharing variables by drawing from donor pools of complete plans (plans where all the cost-sharing questions had been answered) and using only the values required to "fill in" the missing data.

For this to work, the donor pools were subdivided into categories that would be likely to produce a good match (see Table 6). In general, the donor files were defined by sets of other characteristics in common with the record being imputed.

Note that these donor pools are not mutually exclusive: The donor pools could and did overlap, and a donor record could be present in more than one pool, depending on what information was present on the recipient records. This contrasts with the all the other donor pools used for imputation, where the pools were mutually exclusive and where donor records could appear in only one pool.

Despite our care in setting criteria for the donor pool, it was inevitable that imputation would introduce values that violated fairly simple known rules characterizing cost-sharing. For example, the nonpreferred deductible should not be *less* than the preferred deductible. Therefore, extensive post-imputation checking was done to enforce these and other "rules." In fact, the random drawing routines were structured with the assumption that each draw would be done in a loop, with potentially many subsequent draws necessary before a draw abiding by all rules occurred.

Table 6

Donor Pools for Imputing Cost Sharing

HMO	Draw from all clean HMO plans in a single group.
PPO	*Copayment is known* on recipient file: draw stop-loss and deductible from donor pools stratified into 3 groups: copayment=$0, <= $10, or > $10.
	Deductible is known on recipient file: draw stop-loss and copayment from donor pools stratified in 6 groups: no deductible and five quintiles of deductible.
	Copayment and deductible unknown: draw from single pool of all PPOs with complete information.
Indemnity	*Deductible is known* on recipient file: draw from pools stratified into 5 groups: no deductible, four quartiles of deductible.
	Coinsurance rate is known on recipient file: draw from pools with no coinsurance, coinsurance <= 20 percent and > 20 percent (three strata).
	Deductible and coinsurance unknown: draw from single pool of all fee indemnity plans with complete data.

BENEFITS

Coverage for specific plan benefits was imputed for between 3 and 12.4 percent of plans. These benefits include prenatal care, maternity care, outpatient prescription drugs, outpatient mental health services, alcohol and drug treatment, and dental care. Imputation was done using a simple table lookup with cells determined by state and size classes (see Table 5). Random draws determined whether a plan offered the benefit or not.

PREMIUMS

Variables related to premiums or to imputing premiums included the actual premiums for single and family plans, the employer share of each premium, and the proportion of enrollees in family plans. Family enrollment proportions were imputed for 16.2 percent of plans. Single and family premiums were imputed for 29.2 and 25.1 percent of plans, respectively. Employer shares were imputed for between 23.5 and 29.5 percent of plans.

Premiums were flagged as outliers using two sets of criteria: (1) The premiums themselves were subject to high and low cutoff points, and (2) the *ratio* of family premium to single premium was checked. The screen for this ratio required that the family premiums be greater than or equal to the single premium, and not greater than 10 times its amount.

Premiums were imputed using a regression model (see Table 7). There were two basic imputation paths, depending on the pattern of missing premium data on the specific plan record. For cases missing information about premiums for single coverage and family coverage, a family premium was first imputed using a regression model. Then, a family premium-to-single premium ratio was imputed using another regression model with the same variables. Finally, the single premium was calculated by applying the resulting ratio to the family premium. Cases with only one premium missing (family or single) first had the family premium-to-single premium ratio imputed, then had the missing premium value imputed by applying the ratio to the known premium. After calculating a predicted premium value using the regression model, variation was produced by random draws from a pool of residuals. The residuals were derived from the regression model fitted on the nonmissing data. The residual pools were stratified into four size

Table 7

Plan Variables Imputed Using a Regression Model

Dependent variables	single health insurance premium
	family health insurance premium
Independent variables	state
	amount of coinsurance (C22/C23)
	amount of stop-loss (C25)
	type of plan (C3)
	prenatal care (C57a)
	maternity care (C57b)
	outpatient drug prescriptions (C57c)
	outpatient mental health (C57d)
	alcoholism/drug abuse (C57e)
	dental care (C57f)
	exclusion/wait period (C16/C18)
	self-insured status (C14)
	inclusion of administrative costs (C27)
	age and sex distribution of employees (D7)
	establishment size (A1)
	retirees covered? (C49/C44/C32)
	length of waiting period (A27/A28)

categories.[13] Range checking was conducted throughout the premium imputation process. Figure 1 is a simplified flow chart of the premium imputation process.[14]

Some employers were unable to report a separate premium that they were charged for single and family coverage, but were able to report a composite premium—a premium per enrollee that represents a weighted average of costs for single and family coverage. Because we wanted to include a consistent single and family premium for analysis purposes on the research file, we decomposed composite premiums to derive single and family values. This was accomplished by applying the following formulas:

$$P_s = P_c * \frac{1}{[E_s * (1 - R)] + R}$$

$$P_f = P_s * R$$

where

P_f = family premium

P_s = single premium

R = family premium-to-single premium ratio

P_c = composite premium

E_s = proportion enrollees in single plans.

The inclusion of the percentage of enrollees in single plans and the family premium-to-single premium ratio in the above equations necessitated imputing those variables before decomposing the composite premiums. The percentage of single enrollees was imputed only when that variable was unanswered. The family premium-to-single premium ratio had to be imputed for *all* composite premiums.

After completing all the premium imputations, a final editing check was performed on the ratio of total premiums to total payroll. For cases where the ratio of total premiums to total payroll exceeded 50 percent, the establishment was flagged for a final payroll imputation. For these, payroll residuals were redrawn until total premiums no longer exceeded 50 percent of payroll. In

---

[13]The establishment size categories were 1–4, 5–9, 10–24, and 25-plus employees.

[14]It is simplified because it omits many intermediate steps necessary to identify outliers, to create and stratify residual donor pools, and to sort and merge recipient and donor data sets.

essence this meant that a small number of cases that passed the initial payroll screens now *failed* those screens after premium imputation.

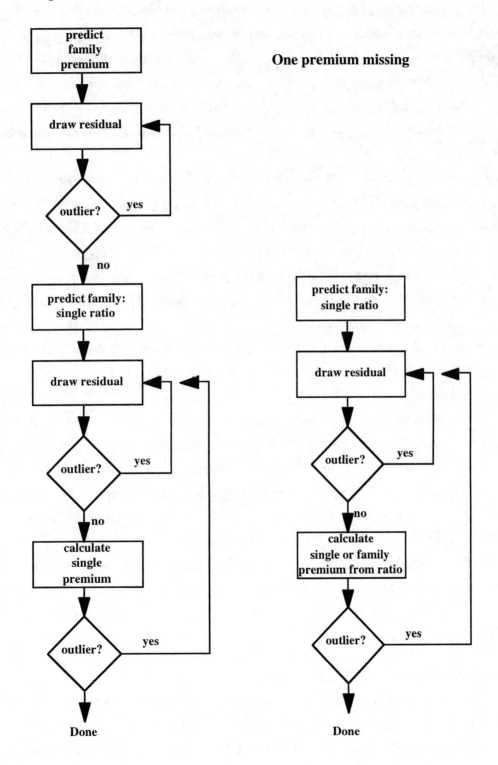

Figure 1—Flow Chart of Premium Imputation

EMPLOYER SHARE OF PREMIUMS

The employer share of the premium was imputed for between 23.5 and 29.2 of plans. Percentages in excess of 100 were eliminated and imputed; these could arise when the employer-share questions were answered in dollar amounts rather than percentages. For self-insured establishments where only employee share was known, or for cases where employer share was missing but employee share was known, employee share was used to determine employer share. In these cases, employee share was subject to a range check to ensure that it did not exceed 100 percent.

Our prevailing assumption for this imputation was that a strong correlation existed between the employer contribution for employees purchasing single coverage and those purchasing family coverage. For example, an employer who paid 100 percent of the premium for single enrollees would be very likely to pay a high percentage of the cost for that plan's family enrollees. Also, we observed that the values were heavily concentrated at percentages ending in 0 or 5, while relatively few employers paid shares ending with other digits (an example would be 73 percent as opposed to 70 or 75 percent). This led us to use a random draw from the donor pool as the imputation method (see Table 4), with the provision that the donor records would include only those cases where *both* employer shares were present. In cases where only one value was missing, only the missing half of the pair was replaced.

For records where both shares were missing, draws were from donor pools stratified by establishment size (two groups), state, and four union/self-insurance categories: union and self-insured, union but not self-insured, self-insured but not union, and neither union nor self-insured. Where only one share was missing, the donor pools were somewhat different: These records were imputed by drawing a record with exactly the same share as the known half of the pair. For example, if family share was exactly 80 percent but single share was missing, a record was randomly drawn from the pool of complete cases where the family shares were also exactly 80 percent. This reflected our notion that pairs of employer shares were strongly correlated within a given plan. For cases where there was no exact matching percentage in the donor data set, the next closest match on either side was used.

PERCENTAGE OF FAMILY ENROLLMENT

The percentage of enrollees in family plans was imputed for 16.2 percent of plans. The imputation was by random draw from a donor pool stratified by four size categories, state, and three family employer-share categories (100 percent, 70–99 percent, less than 70 percent). Note that employer share required imputation before the family enrollment proportion could be imputed (since it was one of the strata for the donor pools).

APPENDIX: IMPUTATION OF MISSING DATA TO PUBLIC EMPLOYERS

We imputed separately for public and private establishments. The distribution of characteristics of public and private workers differs, so it was appropriate to construct different donor pools for the two types of employers. The sample size for public employers was much smaller than for private establishments (543 cases as opposed to 22,347 cases). Therefore, it was not possible to stratify donor pools and hot decks for imputing values to public employers to the same degree as was done for private employers. The key stratifying variable for imputing public employers was "government type." The variable government type had seven categories: federal, state, college or university, and all other governments, classified by the number of employees: 1–49, 50–999, 1000–4999, and 5000 or more. For plan variable imputations, type of plan—HMO, PPO, or conventional—was the additional key stratifying variable. Tables A.1 and A.2 summarize the donor pool stratification used to impute public employer and plan variables, respectively.

There were two other differences in the imputation methods for public and private employers. First, all of the imputations for public employers involved a random draw from a donor pool stratified by government type and/or plan type. Second, several establishment variables were not imputed for the public employers. Annual payroll (D33), number of hours in payroll

Table A.1

Donor Pool Stratification Used to Impute Public "Employer" Variables[a]

Variable	Percent Clean	Stratification Variable: Government Type
Percent permanent employees (A11)	98.5	X
Percent temporary employees (A12)	98.5	X
Number covered employees (A44)	99.8	X
Number former employees covered (A45)	93.7	X
Retirees eligible for coverage (A46)	97.2	X
Retirees <65 eligible for coverage (A47)	97.6	X
Number retirees 65+ covered (A48)	93.0	X
Number retirees <65 covered (A49)	92.8	X

[a]Random draw from stratified donor pools was the methodology used for imputing all variables for public employers. The "employer" or unit of observation includes a group of government agencies or departments whose health insurance plan choices are organized by a common purchasing unit. If a public place of business is not part of a common purchasing pool, it is a separate unit of observation.

Table A.2

Donor Pool Stratification Used to Impute Public Plan Variables

	Percent Clean	Stratification Variables	
		Government Type	Plan Type
Plan type (C3)	94.7	X	
Plan enrollment (C6)	94.4		X
Number former employees enrolled (C7)	55.5		X
Number retirees 65+ enrolled (C8)	60.3		X
Number retirees <65 enrolled (C9)	57.9		X
Family plan offered (C10)	95.1	X	
Number family enrollees (C11)	88.4	X	
Self-insured status (C14)	89.7	X	X
Benefits: plan offers			
Prenatal care (C57a)	93.3	X	
Maternity care (C57b)	93.5	X	
Outpatient drug (C57c)	93.8	X	
Mental health (C57d)	93.0	X	
Alcohol/drugs (C57e)	92.4	X	
Dental care (C57f)	88.3	X	X
Family premium	91.5	X	
Single premium	90.6	X	
Employer share of family premium	83.1		X
Employer share of single premium	89.1		X
Cost sharing variables			
Deductible	93.6	X	
Copay/coinsure	86.6	X	
Stop-loss	84.6	X	
Nonplan services covered	94.9	X	
Deductible (out-of-network)	93.9	X	
Copay/coinsure (out-of-network)	90.3	X	

(D34), age of establishment (D1), and incorporated/nonprofit status (D3, D4) were not included in the questionnaire for public employers. Several variables were not imputed because the values were frequently missing for most of the larger public employers in all states (such as the Federal employer, the state employer) and so suitable donor pools could not be constructed. The number of workers who joined or left in the previous year (D8, D10), the distribution of workers by hours worked (D25 and D26), the distribution by age and sex (D27), and the wage distribution (D29/D31) were not imputed for this reason.